W9-BYD-624

The Who, What, When, Where, Why, and How of Hugging

THE "official"

hugs BOOK ™

HOWARD PUBLISHING CO.

Martha Bolton
ILLUSTRATED BY KRISTY CALDWELL

OUR PURPOSE AT HOWARD PUBLISHING IS TO:

- *Increase faith* in the hearts of growing Christians
- *Inspire holiness* in the lives of believers
- *Instill hope* in the hearts of struggling people everywhere

BECAUSE HE'S COMING AGAIN!

The "Official" Hugs Book © 2002 by Martha Bolton
All rights reserved. Printed in the United States of America

Published by Howard Publishing Co., Inc.
3117 North 7th Street, West Monroe, Louisiana 71291-2227

02 03 04 05 06 07 08 09 10 11   10 9 8 7 6 5 4 3 2 1

Edited by Dawn M. Brandon
Interior design by Stephanie Denney
Illustrations by Kristy Caldwell
Cover design by LinDee Loveland

Library of Congress Cataloging-in-Publication Data
Bolton, Martha, 1951-
    The "official" hugs b[oo]k : the who, what, when, where, why, and how of hugging / Martha Bolton ;
  illustrated by Kristy Caldwell.
        p. cm.
On t. p. "[oo]" appears as 2 hearts.
    ISBN: 1-58229-258-2
  1. Hugging. I. Title.
    BF637.H83 B65 2002
    158.2—dc21

                                                                    2002068507

For Deanne, my favorite

To Sophia King

A godly woman,

a good friend,

and a Hugger Extraordinaire

Love you

Uncle Bill

2003

And to my husband, Russ,

for a lifetime of

flowers,

laughter,

and hugs

Lots of hugs from me!

Contents

♥

In the Beginning Was a Hug 1

The What of Hugging 9

The Why of Hugging 35

The How of Hugging 63

The Who of Hugging 83

The When of Hugging 111

The Where of Hugging 129

The Last Word on Hugging 147

"The greatest gift we can give
one another is rapt attention
to one another's existence."

♥

Sue Atchley Ebaugh

Your very first hug.

> "It is always worthwhile
> to make others aware of their worth."

Malcolm S. Forbes

In the Beginning Was a Hug

• Off to a Good Start •

Your first hug. Not your first hug today, or this week, or even this year, but the first hug of your life. Remember it? Of course you don't. It happened right at the moment of your birth. Someone—the doctor, a midwife, a nurse, your father, your mother, a policeman, a taxi driver, your adoptive parents…someone—cradled you in his or her arms and welcomed you into this world with a hug.

And it surely felt good. After all, you were exhausted from the process of being born. No one had asked you if you wanted to move to another place. You were doing just fine where you were. If it had been up to you, you might have stayed there. But for some reason the process

1

began, and you soon found yourself in a brand-new environment. A place where every face you saw was a new face, and most of them were covered with surgical masks. You probably wondered, *What in the world have I gotten myself into?* Maybe you were a little scared. Maybe you were curious. Maybe you were just too tuckered out to feel anything.

But when that first person lifted you up into loving arms and embraced your new little body, that birth hug instilled in you a feeling of reassurance that you were safe, you were worthwhile, and you were loved. It let you know that even though this new place is different, it's a good place. Not perfect, as you could tell by all the bright lights that made your eyes squint—and from the sting of a firm pat on your bottom that made you cry even if it was to start your breathing on your own. Yes, you were in a different place and quickly discovering that in this world, sometimes a little pain does us good.

That first hug helped you forget the stinging slap and strange lights. All you knew was that you were safe in the haven of someone's arms. When you finally stopped crying, you could hear all the oohs and aahs and excitement over your entry into this world. A welcoming party! *Maybe this being born isn't such a bad idea after all,* you thought.

Fast-forward to today. Whatever your age, you can remember times throughout your life when a hug made you feel loved, worthwhile, comforted, safe, welcome, and special. A hug is powerful. And it's amazing. It's the act of closing your arms around someone to open your heart to them. It's embracing vulnerability and having it embrace you back. It's sharing space, warmth, and worlds, even if only for a moment. It's shelter. It's encouragement. It's validation. It's knowing you can break away, but not wanting to. It's a reminder of every hug that has gone before it and the hope for every hug to come.

A hug has the power to heal broken relationships and wounded spirits. It has even been known to heal physical ailments. A hug is reassurance when we're down, hope in hopeless situations, and the best way to communicate when our words seem inadequate.

The hug. When you think about all it can do, no wonder God felt we all needed to start our lives with one!

• The Origin of the Hug •

The hug must have started with Adam and Eve. Think about it…if you were Adam and had been asking God to give you a helpmate because the animals just weren't that good at conversation, wouldn't you have hugged Eve, God's beautiful answer to your prayer, as soon as you laid eyes on her?

If you were Eve, living in Paradise, never having to worry about football season or dirty socks left on the floor, wouldn't you want to hug the mate for whom you were created?

Of course you would.

And when Eve didn't even get a chance to pack after she and Adam were evicted from the Garden of Eden because of their disobedience, you know she had to have needed a hug then. They were being demoted from Paradise to manual labor, going from a perfect life in the lap of luxury to a rock outside the Garden. Talk about downsizing. And worse yet, Eve would have had to leave most of her new summer wardrobe behind, still hanging on the trees. This was not a good day for her. You'd better believe she needed a hug.

Adam, knowing he was just as responsible for their predicament as Eve was, must have noticed her crying as they walked toward the exit. So, being a loving husband, surely he reached over and gave her a little hug.

In the beginning,
God hugged.

> God is able to make all
>
> grace abound to you,
>
> so that in all things
>
> at all times, having all
>
> that you need,
>
> you will abound
>
> in every good work.
>
> —*2 Corinthians 9:8*

Or maybe not. Maybe they both just played the blame game.

"It's all your fault, Adam!" Eve might have said.

At which point, Adam would have snapped back, "How is it *my* fault?"

"Why didn't you tell me not to listen to that snake?"

"You knew the rules as well as I did."

"Yes, but you know my sweet tooth. Without a Cinnabon in sight, you knew I wouldn't be able to resist! This is your fault, Adam! I was doing just fine until you came along!"

"Hey, wait a minute. Don't twist this around like you always do. God made *me* first!"

"That's *so* like a man to nitpick the details!"

At this point, Adam would have needed a hug!

However it happened, the fact of the matter remains that the first hug likely took place in the Garden. After all, if a hug is anything, it's reassurance when we've messed up. It's comfort when we're feeling all alone. And it's love when we don't feel very lovable.

Adam and Eve knew they had really messed up. Their disobedience had cost them everything. When they realized the predicament they were in, surely they embraced. They probably held on to each other all the way to the exit, now guarded by an angel with a flaming sword.

What Adam and Eve may or may not have realized, though, was that even after their disobedience and shame, God was still hugging them.

"The hunger for love is much more difficult to remove than the hunger for bread."

Mother Teresa

♥

THE What OF HUGGING

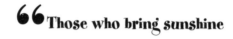

Those who bring sunshine

into the lives of others

cannot keep it from themselves.

James Matthew Barrie

"Love is always open arms."

♥

Leo Buscaglia

What a Hug Is

According to the dictionary, *hug* means "to clasp or hold closely, as with affection; to embrace, to cherish."

That pretty much sums it up, doesn't it? *Hug* is a good word. It's a word that evokes warm memories and instigates high hopes. I hugged, I hug, I will hug. Past, present, future. It can do it all.

Hug is also a nice word. You won't hear it in the middle of a boxing ring: "I'll be floating like a butterfly and stinging like a bee…and maybe I'll give my opponent a little hug just to throw him off." Muhammad Ali would never have said that.

And chances are you won't hear it on too many police dramas: "We've got you surrounded. Come out with your hands up, and let's hug!" A hug might be what the criminal needs, but it still doesn't sound very realistic in that setting, does it?

You won't hear the word *hug* in most suspense or horror films either. Let's face it—a mysterious "I see hugged people" just isn't that scary.

Where you will see hugs is in just about every romantic movie since filmmaking began. You'll also find people hugging at weddings, birthday parties, airports, graduations, family and high school reunions, and hundreds of other places where an embrace just seems to sum up what's on the hearts of everyone.

Sometimes even the long arm of the law can give a hug of mercy.

*Although similar to the untrained eye,
the hug should never be mistaken for the Heimlich maneuver.*

"Do not think that love, in order to be genuine,
has to be extraordinary.
What we need is to love without getting tired."

Mother Teresa

What a Hug Isn't

Although similar to the untrained eye, the hug should never be mistaken for the Heimlich maneuver. While a hug might be comforting to the individual choking on an olive pit, it will do little to dislodge said item from his or her breathing passage. Further, the Heimlich maneuver is usually performed while standing behind someone, putting your arms around him or her, and squeezing until the person is out of danger. The squeezing sensation of a hug may feel similar, but it is almost always done face to face and very rarely involves food (unless you happen to hug a chef).

A hug should not be confused with a tackle, either. The tackle generally takes place on a football field and can involve a dozen or so big, burly guys in shoulder pads. Shoulder pads get in the way of a good hug, and most hugs don't necessitate being taken away on a stretcher afterward.

It should also be noted that hugging is much different from mugging. When you're mugged, chances are you're going to lose all your money. Hugging can cost money, too, but at least you usually know the people going for your wallet (spouse, kids, fund-raising chairmen, etc.).

A hug can also be incorrectly confused with a wrestling move. Wrestlers may look like they're hugging at times, but they seldom are. As a general rule, a hug won't involve the words "You goin' down, sucka! You goin' *down!* My momma didn't raise no wimpy wimps! I'll see you in the ring, me and you, toe to toe! You goin' down!" No matter how tightly their arms may be wrapped around each other, it's definitely *not* a hug.

A scissor hold is not a hug.

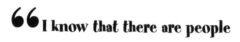**I know that there are people**

who do not love their fellowman,

and I hate people like that!

Tom Lehrer

The most famous hug in the Bible.

> **"People need loving the most
> when they deserve it the least."**

John Harrigan

Famous Hugs of the Bible

• A Father's Hug •

The most famous hug in the Bible, no doubt, is the one found in the parable of the prodigal son. Here was a son who had squandered everything his father had given him. He had acted pridefully, ungratefully, shortsightedly, and selfishly. After making a string of bad decisions and hitting rock bottom, he finally came to the conclusion that it was time to go home. After all, why should he have to sleep with dirty pigs, scrounging around for a morsel of something to eat, while the hired hands at his father's estate were eating three squares a day?

Truly repentant, the son gathered up what strength he had left and started for home. He didn't care whether or not he received a son's

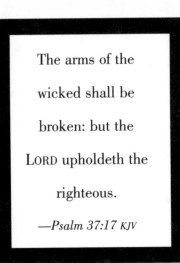

The arms of the wicked shall be broken: but the LORD upholdeth the righteous.

—*Psalm 37:17 KJV*

welcome. He knew he didn't deserve one. He only hoped that his father would have enough love and forgiveness to treat him as well as one of the hired workers.

But that's not what happened.

When the father saw his estranged son approaching, he ran to him and threw his arms around him. Translated, that means "He hugged him, and he hugged him, and he hugged him." Then he kissed him and ordered his servants to bring his finest robe and to prepare a celebratory feast. Translated, that means "It's party time!"

Think about what that hug meant to the prodigal son—and what it means to us. The hug of that father meant...

I love you.

I've always loved you.

I forgive you.

You are my child.

I've been waiting for your return.

You've been on my mind continually.

There's nothing I wouldn't do for you.

You're beautiful.

Leave the cleaning up to me.

It's time to celebrate!

My joy is complete.

Welcome home. No details necessary.

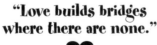

**"Love builds bridges
where there are none."**

R. H. Delaney

• A Brother's Hug •

Another famous hug mentioned in the Bible is one of those difficult hugs. You know, the kind where the recipient doesn't really deserve a hug, but you give it anyway.

Joseph was a young boy who was hated by his brothers. Why did they hate him? Because he picked fights with them? Because he was inconsiderate and mean? No. Joseph's brothers hated him because he was good.

Say what?

It's true. Joseph's brothers were jealous of him. Joseph was loved by his father, so his brothers hated him. He was kind and considerate, so they hated him. He had a calling on his life, so they hated him. He was trusting, so they threw him into a pit, then later sold him into slavery...and they still hated him.

But God would not allow His plan for Joseph to be thwarted by a bunch of jealous brothers. In fact, their evil deeds played right into God's plan. Joseph ended up being taken to Egypt and, after a long

A hug of forgiveness.

> He threw his arms
> around his brother
> Benjamin and wept,
> and Benjamin
> embraced him,
> weeping. And he
> kissed all his
> brothers and wept
> over them.
> Afterward his
> brothers talked
> with him.
>
> —*Genesis 45:14–15*

chain of God-directed events, became second in command over all of Egypt.

When a drought struck the region, Joseph's brothers were forced to come to Egypt for grain—and guess who was in charge of doling out the grain? Their long-lost brother, Joseph. After playing them along for a while, a tearful Joseph finally revealed his identity.

The brothers certainly didn't deserve a hug, but Joseph gave one to them anyway. A hug of forgiveness. A hug of reconciliation. A hug that only God could have orchestrated.

"Fear less, hope more;
Whine less, breathe more;
Talk less, say more;
Hate less, love more;
And all good things are yours."

Swedish Proverb

• A Child's Hug •

Remember when Jesus called the little children to Himself and hugged them? He then told His disciples that unless they changed and became like little children, they couldn't enter the kingdom of heaven. What He was saying was that He wanted them to have childlike faith, childlike trust, and childlike love.

Hugs come naturally to children. They see their mom and dad standing at the school gate, waiting to pick them up, and they run as fast as they can to give them a hug. They know a hug means "I love you!"

They also know a hug brings comfort. A little boy skins his knee; he wants a hug. A little girl loses her balloon; she wants a hug. A child's pet mouse escapes from its cage, and the child needs a hug (and help catching the mouse). Children know that hugs make them feel better. They make the boo-boos of life go away.

Unfortunately, as we grow older, we forget the benefits of hugging. Some of us begin to think of hugging as undignified, so we put up a wall. We think it will invade our personal space, so we put up a wall. We think it'll wrinkle our clothes, so we put up a wall.

In the end, what do we have? Perfectly pressed clothes and a lot of walls.

Try to recall how—as a child—you blindly trusted your parents. Remember the uninhibited love that made you run full-speed into their arms. And how about all those squeeze-tight hugs—the ones you wanted to go on forever?

That's how Jesus wants us to love Him—with childlike abandon.

Childlike abandon.

The Language of Hugs

A hug says EVERYTHING WILL BE FINE...
when you can't find the words.

A hug says I'M SORRY...
when words can't be heard.

A hug says THANK YOU...
> when words aren't enough.

A hug says I'VE MISSED YOU...
> when words would just get in the way.

A hug says I'M PROUD OF YOU...
> when you can't speak the words.

A hug says YOU CAN DO IT...
> when words seem inadequate.

A hug says I LOVE YOU...
> when that says it all.

A Hug in Any Language

ENGLISH
"I need a hug."

PIG LATIN
"I eednay a ughay."

SPANISH
"Necesito un abrazo."

GERMAN
"Ich benötige eine
Umarmung."

VALLEY
"Like, give me a
hug, okaaay?"

BLUES
"Slap me some arms, man!"

ITALIAN
"Ho bisogno di un hug."

FRENCH
"J'ai besoin d'une étreinte."

SURFER
"Hey, dude. Whatzup with my hug?"

PREACHER
"I see that hand. I see that other hand.
Now wrap them around the person next to you
and give him or her a hug."

According to the Guinness Book of World Records,

the largest hug on record took place in October 2001 in the United States and involved 2,903 people!

Neither death nor life,

neither angels nor demons,

neither the present nor the future,

nor any powers,

neither height nor depth,

nor anything else in all creation,

will be able to separate us from the love of God

that is in Christ Jesus our Lord.

—Romans 8:38–39

How U Get Squeezed

"Tell me who admires you and loves you,
and I will tell you who you are."

Charles Augustin Sainte-Beuve

♥

THE why OF HUGGING

> "To love a person means to see him
> as God intended him to be."

♥

Fyodor Dostoevsky

Top Ten Reasons for Hugging

1. The world needs it.

All you have to do is watch the evening news to know that our world is suffering from a dangerous shortage of love. Terrorism, riots, wars, school shootings—the stories of crimes against humanity fill our nightly newscasts and our minds. And our children's minds.

The world isn't a pretty place. It was at one time, but then man came on the scene, and look what we've done with the place. Don't get me wrong—we've accomplished a lot of good. But few would say that we as a society love each other enough.

Not that a few more hugs will make all the bad things go away. Not

A hug makes you take flight.

even a few million more hugs. People have free will to do what they please, and some may never choose to change.

But a little more love for our fellowman certainly couldn't hurt.

Love has power. It can change a heart, a circumstance, even a life. Change enough lives, and we'll eventually change society.

A hug can do that? Well, it's a gradual process, and it won't change everyone—but it can make a difference.

 The biggest disease

in this day and age

 is that of people

feeling unloved.

Author Unknown

2. You need it.

The best thing about hugging is that the hugger benefits, too.

You can't give away love without getting some of it back. A hug makes us feel better about ourselves, about the other person, and about our situation. Whether it's a farewell, an illness, a tragedy, a hurt, a misunderstanding, or a job loss, hugs benefit both the giver and the receiver.

Hugs benefit both
the giver and the receiver.

3. It's healing.

Yes, hugs even have medicinal benefits. If you don't believe me, just watch an injured child's tears dry up in the circle of a mother's or father's embrace. Watch a new mother forget all about the pain of birth after snuggling that beautiful new baby. And watch an old man barely clinging to life suddenly light up with renewed strength and a will to live when his estranged son or daughter walks into the room and embraces him.

Hugs have medicinal benefits.

 Forgiveness does

not change the past,

but it does

enlarge the future.

Paul Boese

It's generally accepted that huggers look younger than nonhuggers.

4. It's age defying.

There's no scientific study or anything like that to prove this theory, but it's generally accepted that huggers look younger than nonhuggers. The reason is simple—when you add a little more love to your life, you leave less room for stress. And stress is aging. So if you're looking for that fountain of youth, you just may find it in a hug.

66Age does not protect you from love,

but love to some extent protects you from age.**99**

Jeanne Moreau

66 If someone listens, or stretches out a hand,

or whispers a kind word of encouragement,

or attempts to understand a lonely person,

extraordinary things begin to happen. **99**

Loretta Girzartis

5. It's contagious.

Remember the final episode of *The Mary Tyler Moore Show* when the entire cast said good-bye in one big, tearful group hug? And how, not wanting to break the embrace, they moved as one unit toward the desk with a box of tissues on it? It's a classic bit that most of us didn't see coming and will never forget.

Hugs are contagious. It takes only one person to start a hugfest, and before you know it, a whole roomful of people will stop the formality of shaking hands and move full speed ahead into hugging.

Are there people in your life who could use a hug today? Could you use a hug? Starting a hug chain takes only one person—why not let it start with you?

Need a hug? Take a hug. Got a hug? Give a hug.

6. It's fun.

A hug makes you feel good. It can make you feel like a kid again. It's like when you were a child and would run into your mother's or father's arms after an amusement-park ride and beg, "Can I do it again? Can I, huh? Can I?" A hug can remind you of when your father held you in his strong and loving arms as he taught you to swim and, in the

A hug means good memories.

process, you learned to trust. Or when your mother embraced you as you blew out the candles on your tenth birthday cake. A hug means good memories of fun, laughter, and joy—past, present, and future.

"He who laughs, lasts."

Mary Pettibone Poole

7. Any of us can do it.

Hugging doesn't take a lot of practice. It's a natural talent born inside each one of us. If you can open your arms and close them again, you can hug.

Anyone can hug.

> **"Love means to love that which is unlovable;
> or it is no virtue at all."**

♥

G. K. Chesterton

8. God told us to.

Throughout the Bible, we are told to love one another—including
the unlovely. It's a commandment just like all the "Thou shalt nots,"
only this is something we *should* do. Sometimes it's hard.

Let's face it—there are people in this world, in your church, maybe
even in your family who make it difficult to love them. It's like trying
to hug a shark. They may let you do it, but it's hard to ignore the size of
their bite.

Yet God said to love them. We don't have to approve of their
behavior. We don't have to trust them to return our kindness with
love. But we do have to love them. That's our part. Changing their
hearts is God's part.

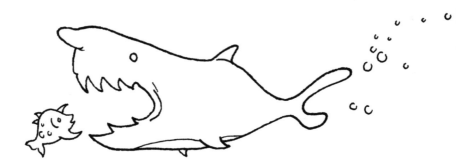

Some people make it difficult to love them.

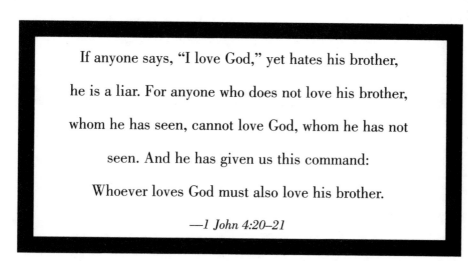

If anyone says, "I love God," yet hates his brother,

he is a liar. For anyone who does not love his brother,

whom he has seen, cannot love God, whom he has not

seen. And he has given us this command:

Whoever loves God must also love his brother.

—1 John 4:20–21

9. It keeps us busy.

It's hard to be mean to someone when our arms are wrapped around him or her. It's hard to judge, discourage, ridicule, or hate. When we're that close to another human being, most of us say nice things. We tend to drop feelings of competition, hurt, envy, pride, and hatred and give way to feelings of compassion, forgiveness, understanding, acceptance, and mercy. Hugging keeps us busy thinking the right things.

Do not judge, and you will not be judged.

Do not condemn, and you will not be condemned.

Forgive, and you will be forgiven.

—*Luke 6:37*

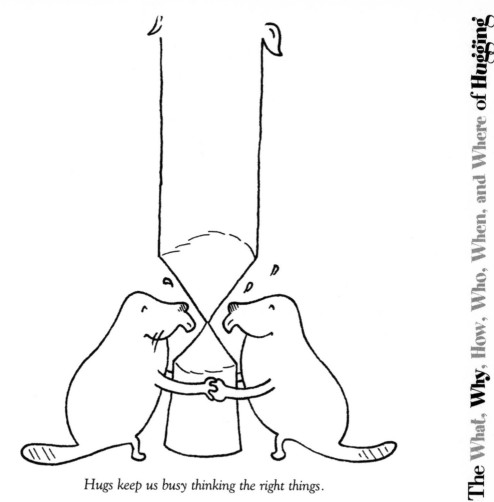

Hugs keep us busy thinking the right things.

If you're going to show someone
how much you love her,
do it now.

10. We only have so much time.

Each one of us has only been given a short time here on earth. If we're going to hug someone, if we're going to tell others how much they mean to us, if we're going to show them how much we love them, we need to do it now. Not next Christmas. Not this summer. Not tomorrow. Today.

"The way to love anything
is to realize that it might be lost."

G. K. Chesterton

Hugs as Therapy

Problem	Prescription
Bad hair day	2 hugs
Discouraging remark	4 hugs
Rude salesclerk	6 hugs

Aggressive motorist ....5 hugs

Rush-hour traffic ....7 hugs

Air travel ....8 hugs

Unexpected bill ....3 hugs

IRS audit ....9 hugs

Mother-in-law visit..................20 hugs

"If you judge people,
you have no time to
love them."

Mother Teresa

 Love is not blind—it sees more,

not less. But because it sees

more, it is willing to see less. "

Rabbi Julius Gordon

Though he stumble,

he will not fall,

for the LORD upholds him with his hand.

—*Psalm 37:24*

Hugging as Exercise

If one hug burns 3 calories,

then hugging 20 people a day is equivalent to:

9 MINUTES
of stair-stepping

8.5 MINUTES
of aerobics

8 MINUTES
of jogging

7 MINUTES
of tennis

6 MINUTES
of racquetball

5 MINUTES
of weight-lifting

Now which sounds like more fun to you?

(Note: Calculations are only estimates

and not meant for scientific use.)

If one hug burns 3 calories, then

hugging 20 people

a day is equivalent to:

7 minutes of tennis.

Arms Control:

The ability of politicians
to refrain from hugging

**Small things,**

done in great love,

bring joy and peace.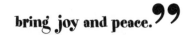

Mother Teresa

THE how OF HUGGING

"Too many are waiting for God
to do something *for* them rather than *with* them."

♥

Ralph W. Sockman

The Ten
Most Common
Ways to Hug

Now that we know what a hug is and isn't, that it's been around a long time, and even how to ask for one in ten different languages, let's discuss *how* we hug. There are many ways to hug. Here are the ten most common.

1. The Boa Constrictor Hug

This is the mother of all hugs. Like the reptile of the same name, the Boa Constrictor Hug is a friendly but forceful squeeze that tightens around the recipient more with each passing moment. Locked in this powerful hug, the "huggee" will find it virtually impossible to get away, so he or she might as well relax and enjoy it.

2. The Grizzly Bear Hug

This hug was named after the grizzly bear, even though grizzly bears don't technically "hug" people (the proper word might be *attack*). The Grizzly Bear Hug is that cuddly hug that most of us love to receive. It's warm and snuggly, and it makes you feel safe, secure, and very, very loved.

3. The Embrace

The Embrace is the most romantic of all hugs. This is done by a couple, to show affection toward each other. It can be done in public or in private, on special occasions or on an ordinary day. The Embrace has been known to mend hurts, solve disagreements, and make a spouse forget all about that freshly dented car fender. (Well, almost.)

4. The Aunt Thelma Hug

If you're an adult with a fear of hugging, this is probably the hug that did it to you. The Aunt Thelma Hug has been known to affect children into adulthood and for the rest of their natural lives. If you've ever received one of these hugs, you understand. The Aunt Thelma is the hug that buried your six-year-old face into Aunt Thelma's ample stomach with no clear path of oxygen while she tousled your hair and talked about how much you'd grown. Like a Stephen King film, the mere memory of this hug can keep you awake at night (and keep you away from family reunions for years).

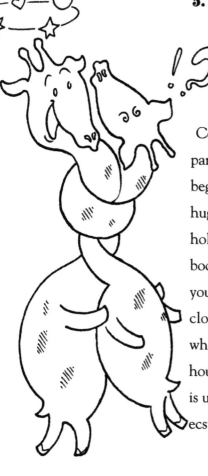

5. The Main Squeeze

If you can't imagine what a tube of toothpaste feels like every morning, then you've never been subjected to the Main Squeeze. Unlike the Boa Constrictor Hug, which can start at any part of your body, the Main Squeeze usually begins at your waist. Once engaged, the hugger will proceed to tighten his or her hold on you, steadily redistributing your body fat to parts unknown. After the hug, you won't be able to fit into any of your clothes until your body readjusts itself, which has been known to take up to several hours. Like the Aunt Thelma Hug, this hug is usually performed by distant relatives and ecstatic game-show winners.

6. The Cheek-to-Cheek Hug

This is the hug in which you actually touch cheeks with the other person. The length of this popular hug depends on the amount of garlic consumed in the previous twenty-four-hour period and the length of a participant's beard stubble.

7. The Straitjacket Hug

This is the overly enthusiastic hug you receive from someone before you've had a chance to open your own arms. This often happens when you're carrying a load of packages and run into an old friend at the mall. It's a sincere hug, but it can be quite uncomfortable, depending on the position of the corners of your shopping boxes.

8. Hug Lite

The Hug Lite is what you receive when the hugger is busy doing something else. The person's mind really isn't on hugging, but he or she does it anyway. A Hug Lite can also be given to people you don't really know but feel obligated to hug (e.g., when you're attending a Poison Oak Victims fund-raiser and the speaker tells the audience to "Go hug your neighbor").

Do not fear, for I am with you; do not be dismayed,

for I am your God. I will strengthen you and help you;

I will uphold you with my righteous right hand.

—Isaiah 41:10

9. The Morning-Breath Hug

Unlike other hugs, this one is usually given from across the room. The huggers reach their arms outward and mime a hug. There is no physical contact, just an emotional one. This hug is not intended to replace a real hug. It's merely a precursor to a genuine hug that will come later in the day (usually after some mouthwash).

10. The Superhero Hug

This is the hug that arrives just in the nick of time. From the moment you rolled out of bed in the morning, your day has been like a beginning ski lesson—everything headed downhill and none of it pretty. But just when you're feeling your worst, when you're thinking that if one more thing goes wrong, it'll be your undoing, someone comes along and gives you a much needed hug.

You didn't ask for it. You just got it. No strings attached. No sermons on why you didn't do this right or that better. It's just a hug to remind you that you're loved. In all of hugdom, there is none better.

**"The comforter's head
never aches."**

♥

Italian Proverb

Heart Hugs

Not all hugging involves touch. Sometimes, because of circumstances, you have to do your hugging from across the room, across town, or even across many miles. Does that make the hug any less special? Of course not. It just makes it a Heart Hug.

Heart Hugs come in all shapes and sizes. A Heart Hug can be between a soldier and his family back home. It can be between a lonely, confused teenager and his father through the cold, impersonal glass of a prison visitation area. A Heart Hug might be from a boy dedicating a song on the radio to the girl he just met who lives on the other side of town. It can be between a mother and her cancer-ridden son who's in isolation because of the high dosage of chemotherapy.

Heart Hugs are so strong they don't need an embrace to be felt.

Sometimes, because of circumstances,
you have to do your hugging across many miles.

Welcome! You've Got Hugs!

One way to send a Heart Hug is via the Internet. It's a great feeling to find one of these messages waiting for you, isn't it? They're fun to send, too. Here are a few symbols you might want to use in your next e-hug.

< > or ( )
E-MAIL HUG

((( )))
E-MAIL GROUP HUG

>0 0<

TWO HUGGERS WHO HAVEN'T **0< >0**
YET FOUND EACH OTHER

TWO HUGGERS PREPARING TO HUG

0< >0 0< >0 0< >0

A HUGGERS CONVENTION

OX XO

TWO NONHUGGERS MEETING

OX XO OX XO OX XO

A NONHUGGERS CONVENTION

8<

A CALIFORNIA HUGGER WEARING SUNGLASSES

0< XO

A HUGGER MEETING A NONHUGGER

Coat of Arms:
What a hugger wears in the winter

66 Hold a true friend

with both your hands. **99**

Nigerian Proverb

THE who
OF HUGGING

*Brushing against each other in front of the
bathroom mirror is nice, but it isn't a hug.*

"Do all things with love."

♥

Og Mandino

Who You Should Hug

• Your Spouse

Couples should hug at least once every day. Brushing against each other in the hallway or in front of the bathroom mirror is nice, but it doesn't constitute a hug. A real hug is at least ten seconds long.

A hug of that length doesn't leave you wondering...

Did he hug me, or was he just moving me out of the way of the TV?

Was I just hugged, or was she brushing the lint off my jacket?

Ten-second hugs (or better yet, twenty- and thirty-second hugs) leave no doubt. And in this day and age, who needs doubt? Life's tough. Couples have to face a lot of frustrations. So take a hug break and hold on to that one you love just a little bit tighter, just a little bit longer, and see if it doesn't change your outlook on the day.

66 The supreme happiness in life

is the conviction that we are loved–

loved for ourselves, or rather,

loved in spite of ourselves. 99

Victor Hugo

• Your Children

Children are a gift from the Lord. It may not seem like it when you discover the cherry lollipop stuck to the elbow of your new suit, but it's true. Children are a blessing. And they require a steady diet of hugs. Hugs tell children that they're better than the spilled milk, the unfinished homework, the unmade bed, and the fights with their siblings over toys or over who gets to control the remote. Hugs reassure children that they're loved simply because of who they are.

Hugs reassure children that they're loved simply because of who they are.

• Your Parents

Parenting is hard work. Even after a child is all grown up, parents are still parents. They still want the best for their children. They still want to defend them against insensitive, discouraging people. They still want to be there when their children need a shoulder to lean on. They still want to communicate their faith in them. They still want them to know they're loved and appreciated and valued. Parenting doesn't stop when a son or daughter hits a certain birthday or says "I do."

A parent's love is forever, a parent's concern is forever, and a parent will always be ready to give a hug. And after all this, certainly parents also need and deserve hugs from their children!

A parent's love is forever.

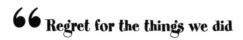 Regret for the things we did

can be tempered by time;

it is regret for the things

we did not do that is inconsolable.

Sydney J. Harris

• Your Grandparents

A grandparent's love is one of the most unconditional forms of love there is. Grandparents are forgiving, fun, honest, unpretentious, and usually great cooks. They also have that prized possession—time. Grandparents are never too busy to hug you. And they're great huggers! They're always ready to wrap you in their arms and give you a grandparent-sized hug. When was the last time you took a few minutes to hug your grandparents?

Grandparents are open for hugs 24/7.

• Your Friends

Friend-hugs are the warmest. Friends are people who don't have to love you—they just do. They don't have to hug you—they just want to. A real friend knows when you need a hug even before you ask for it, even before you think you need it, and even when no one else is offering it.

Friends don't let friends go unhugged.

"To love another person is to see the face of God."

Victor Hugo

A pet will be there when no one else is.

• Your Pet

Unconditional love. If you don't get it from anyone else in your life, you'll get it from your pet. A pet will be there for you when no one else is. Pets will be in your corner when you're alone, with the weight of the world on your shoulders. They'll defend you, love you, and let you hug them whenever you need to. Even cats, which don't lend their affections easily, will respond to a warm and friendly hug from their human friends.

> ### "Always love your enemies—
> ### nothing annoys them so much."
>
> ♥
>
> **Oscar Wilde**

• Your Enemies

Hug an enemy? That must be a misprint. What in the world would I want to do that for?

Well, think about it—what would surprise your enemies more than opening your arms and giving them a big hug? After all, God tells us to love them. Loving them will pre-serve our own peace of mind. The act of hugging them might even leave them speechless...and just think how nice that would be!

What would surprise your enemies more than opening your arms and giving them a hug?

Give yourself a hug—discover who you are;
explore your dreams.

"If you aren't good at loving yourself,
you will have a difficult time loving anyone,
since you'll resent the time and energy you give another person
that you aren't even giving to yourself."

Barbara De Angelis

• Yourself

It doesn't matter how many people you hug throughout the day if you're not giving a few self-hugs in the process. A self-hug isn't an exercise in which you wrap your arms around your shoulders and squeeze yourself into unconsciousness. Giving a self-hug is loving yourself. It's being interested in discovering who you are, your interests, your desires, your dreams. It's caring for yourself.

Too often we put ourselves so far down on the hug chain that we can't help but feel taken advantage of. But more often than not, we're the ones taking the most advantage of us.

Give yourself a hug today. If you love yourself—not in an inflated ego kind of way but in a nurturing, loving way—others can't help but follow suit.

Popular Songs for Huggers

The Nearness of You

Put Your Head on
My Shoulder

(Let Me Be Your) Teddy Bear

Embrace Me

Loving Arms

Time on My Hands
(And You in My Arms)

Put Your Arms Around Me,
Honey

Sometimes When We Touch

Wrapped Up, Tied Up,
Tangled All Up with Jesus

Huggers' Bumper Stickers

I Brake for Hugs

Only the Hugged Survive

Stand Up and Be Hugged!

I Hug...Therefore I Am

My Child Is a Hugged Student

If You're Close Enough to Read This, We Might As Well Hug

...got hugs?

"He drew a circle that shut me out
Heretic, rebel, a thing to flout
But love and I had the wit to win;
We drew a circle that took him in."

Edwin Markham

Hugophobia:
The fear of being hugged

Who You Should Not Hug

⊘ Never hug a two-year-old who's been eating a butterscotch sundae as finger food unless you're wearing a full-body bib.

⊘ Never hug your personal trainer while using the treadmill unless it's the only way to get your brownies back.

⃠ **Never hug your husband during the last forty-five seconds of the Super Bowl**

when the score is tied

and his team has the ball on the

three-yard line...

unless

you like

seeing a

grown

man

cry.

⊘ Never hug a pregnant woman during the last four minutes of a twenty-three-hour labor, especially if you're her husband. Be there for her and encourage her, but stay out of swinging range until the labor is over and the beautiful little bundle has arrived.

⊘ **Never hug your doctor during surgery,** no matter how brilliantly he or she is performing. Keep your eyes closed and pretend you're still under anesthesia.

○ **Never hug a waiter
who's balancing
five dinner plates
on his head...**

**unless
you look good
in roast beef.**

⊘ **Never hug
someone
across the table**
at a wedding reception...
especially if there's
an ice sculpture
between you.

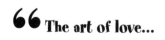 The art of love...

is largely

the art of persistence.

Albert Ellis

Popular Songs for Nonhuggers

Please Release Me

Even a Fool Would Let Go

How Can I Miss You If You Won't Go Away?

Let Me Go, Lover

Prisoner of Love

I'll Have to Say I Love You in a Song

Movies for Nonhuggers

A Farewell to Arms

Force of Arms

Armed and Dangerous

Nonhuggers' Mascot:

Venus de Milo

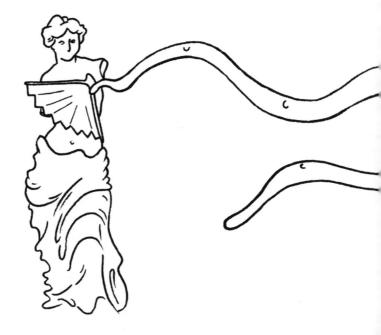

Huggers' Mascot:

The octopus

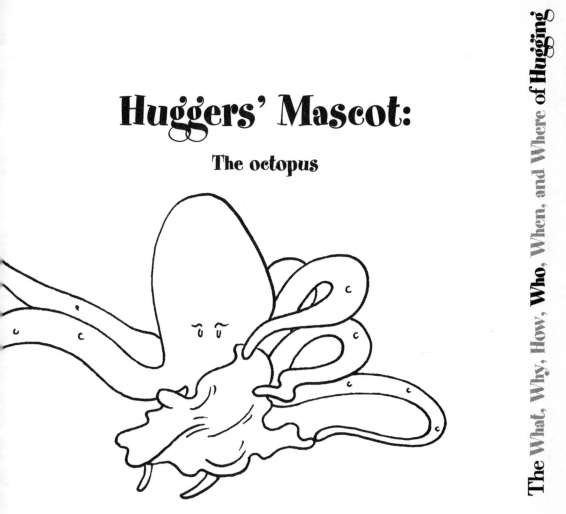

THE when OF HUGGING

**"At the touch of love
everyone becomes a poet."**

Plato

Top Ten Occasions
for Hugging

1. Valentine's Day

Out of all the holidays on the calendar, Valentine's Day is by far the huggingest day. Everyone is in the mood to show love. Husbands and wives, boyfriends and girlfriends, brothers and sisters, parents and children, fathers and sons, friends, and maybe even a few dogs and cats find themselves getting along a little better on Cupid's big day.

> ...a time to embrace.
>
> —*Ecclesiastes 3:5*

Valentine's Day is by far the huggingest day.

2. Any Birthday after 40

Another occasion on which a hug is the order of the day is at any birthday party involving 40 or more candles on the cake. An after-40 birthday man or woman needs emotional support like never before. A hug can make the person feel needed, loved, and appreciated. And the best thing about an over-40 hug is, if the recipient forgets that you just gave one, you get to give another.

Any birthday involving 40 or more candles is an occasion for a hug.

3. Bad Hair Day

We've all had them. From the moment we crawl out of bed in the morning, it seems everything that could possibly go wrong does. This kind of a day screams for a hug. A hug, like a certain bubble bath advertises, is waiting to "take you away." You'll probably still have your troubles afterward, just as you do after a bath; but the hug certainly couldn't hurt. Let's face it, life just doesn't seem quite as overwhelming after a little TLC (Tender Loving Cuddle).

This kind of day screams for a hug.

4. Driving-Test Day

A celebratory hug is always in order when your teenager passes the driving test. You hug to let your son or daughter know you're proud, you hug to encourage, you hug to show support, and you hug because as long as those adolescent arms are wrapped around you, they won't be able to grab the car keys.

As long as those adolescent arms are wrapped around you,
they won't be able to grab the car keys.

One final hug.

5. April 15–Income-Tax Day

Before saying good-bye forever, many people want to give their money one long, final hug.

6. Mother's Day

No one has worked harder for her day of hugs than a mother. She deserves it! She needs it, too. A hug is a huge energy boost for a mom. It's bonus pay. A tip. Validation. A gift. It's what she lives for and what she'll always hope for. She can never get enough hugs, yet she'll continue doing what she does whether she gets one or not. That's a mom.

Moms live *for hugs*.

*Dads don't always
get the recognition they deserve.*

7. Father's Day

Even if a dad doesn't ask for hugs, you can be sure he wants them.
And more often than just on Father's Day. Dads don't always get the
recognition they deserve, but on Father's Day we all stop to pay tribute
to the man who bears the title of Dad. Friend. Counselor. Hero.

8. Graduation Day

When you think of all the late nights you spent helping your child with homework; all the money you spent on tuition, books, and collect calls; when you remember the worrying and the calls from the principal or dean—you'll agree that if anyone deserves a hug on graduation day, you do! (And so does your son or daughter!)

If anyone deserves a hug on graduation day, parents do.

9. Christmas

Even if your clan makes the Addams Family look like the Cleavers, Christmas is a day for hugs. The very reason for Christmas is love. God loved the world so much that He sent us His Son, Jesus. So you can't celebrate Christmas and not talk about love. You can't sing carols, drink eggnog, saw your way through Aunt Thelma's fruitcake, decorate the tree, or open gifts and not hug one another.

Christmas love is what helps you put up with Uncle Harry, who hides his teeth in the fruit bowl, and Aunt Mary, who keeps wandering outside and talking to the plastic reindeer on the roof. Faith. Family. And hugs. They're what Christmas is all about.

Christmas means love—even when you have to saw through Aunt Thelma's fruit cake.

10. Close Calls

There's nothing quite like the hug you give just after you've been granted a second chance at life. You've survived a close call (a serious car accident, a life-threatening disease, my cooking…), and now you can't help yourself—you want to hug everyone on the planet. You have a renewed appreciation for life and your loved ones. This is a perfectly normal reaction to a near-death experience, and this kind of hug is by far one of the most sincere and meaningful.

After you survive a close call, you want to hug everyone on the planet.

We love

because he

first loved us.

—*1 John 4:19*

Arms Race:

Seeing who'll be the first to offer a hug

66 You will find as you look back upon your life

that the moments when you have truly lived

are the moments when you

have done things in the spirit of love. 99

Henry Drummond

> **"God loves each of us
> as if there were only one of us."**
>
> ♥
>
> **St. Augustine**

A God-Timed Hug

Have you ever gotten a hug at exactly the right time? God knows the precise moment when you need a hug. He knows when you're feeling beaten up by life—when you don't think you can last another second, much less another round.

And His timing is perfect. A well-timed hug comes just when we

> The LORD upholds all
> those who fall and
> lifts up all who are bowed down.
>
> —*Psalm 145:14*

need it, often from an unexpected source. That's the part about God that always amazes me. While we're waiting for the people we expect to encourage us, He sends someone along who doesn't even know what we're going through. Some-one who just feels like hugging us. That's when there's no doubt in our mind Who's behind the hug. It's a God Hug.

Just *one* of these special hugs can restore your faith and give you the strength to go on. In fact, the shelf life of a hug like this can be years. Maybe even decades.

Saved by a hug.

THE where

OF HUGGING

10 Most Popular Places to Hug

1. At your front door

(The first place to greet relatives, neighbors, and mailmen

who bring you unexpected checks.)

2. At the mall

(It'll keep your spouse's hands busy so he or she can't reach for the credit card.)

3. At the hospital

(Should you become entangled in the IV tubing, don't panic.
Simply ring for the nurse and continue to hug until help arrives.)

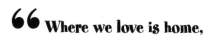 **Where we love is home,**

home that our feet may leave,

but not our hearts.

Oliver Wendell Holmes

4. At high-school reunions

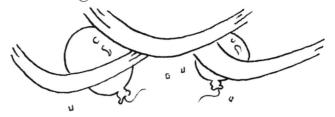

(It's the best way to get close enough to tell
which ones still have their own hair.)

5. At church

(When the preacher says, "Get out of your seat and go hug
your neighbor," that's the perfect time to
go reclaim your usual pew from those visitors.)

6. At the grocery store

(It'll keep you warm in the frozen-food aisle.)

7. In a maternity ward after the birth of the baby

(It makes up for everything the mother said during labor.)

8. At election-night political rallies

(But it's wise to keep one hand on your wallet at all times.)

9. At airports—whether you're saying "good-bye" or "welcome home"

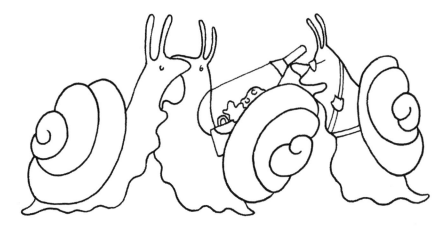

(Security-guard frisking doesn't count.)

10. At the bowling alley after a strike

(But put the ball down first. It could break a rib.)

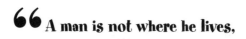 **A man is not where he lives,**

but where he loves.

Latin Proverb

How Far Would You Go for a Hug?

18 inches...

To hug that person in the pew behind you who just belted out the first three bars of "Amazing Grace" while the rest of the congregation was singing "A Mighty Fortress Is Our God"?

2 feet...

To hug the toddler who just spilled cookie crumbs on your computer?

4 feet...

To hug your spouse, who's sitting in silence across the breakfast table from you, freshly wounded from your latest disagreement?

10 feet...

To walk across a crowded foyer and give your pastor an encouraging hug, even in the middle of a building program?

5 miles...

Across town to hug a former best friend who let you down?

500 miles...

To hug the estranged father you haven't seen in years?

10,000 miles...

To hug a hungry child in a foreign land?

To the ends of the earth...

To hug the runaway teenager who left home months ago?

How far would you go for a hug?

Surely I am with you always,

to the very end of the age.

—Matthew 28:20

66 Every day I live I am more convinced

that the waste of life

lies in the love we have not given,

the powers we have not used,

the selfish prudence that will risk nothing

and which, shirking pain, misses happiness as well. **99**

Mary Cholmondeley

> **"While we are postponing, life speeds by."**
>
> ♥
>
> **Seneca**

The Last Word on Hugging

• Last Hugs •

When my mother was diagnosed with lymphoma and given only one month to live if she didn't start chemotherapy right away, I was devastated. It didn't seem real. Or fair. My mother had done so much for so many people. She was a giver. Why did this have to happen to her? *How* could this have happened to her? Until then, my mother had hardly been sick a day in her life. At seventy-two, she was going on her third retirement. The building in which she worked had changed hands three times, and she had been hired by each new company. It was like she had been named in escrow.

But a career wasn't everything to my mom. I was the youngest of five

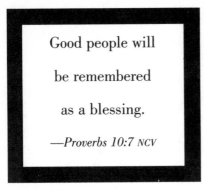

Good people will

be remembered

as a blessing.

—*Proverbs 10:7* NCV

kids, and she would have done anything for any of us. When I was in high school, she served as PTA president while still holding down her full-time job. Mom was incredible.

Now she was fighting for her life.

I remember that during her battle with cancer, our hugs became more meaningful, more lingering. I wanted to hug her and capture the feeling of her breath on my cheek. I knew that one day, I hoped it wouldn't be for years to come, those hugs and the feeling of her breath would be only a memory. I wanted to engrave that memory into my mind.

My mother lived another eight months. During that time we shared plenty of laughs, a lifetime of memories, and a whole lot of hugs. Losing her was one of the most difficult things I've had to face. But now, whenever I miss her, I recall the warmth of those hugs and the feeling of her breath on my cheek.

The Last Word on Hugging

Huggers' Rules of Engagement

1. A hugger shall be available to hug at a moment's notice.

2. Hugs lasting less than one second are "huggettes" and do not constitute real hugs.

3. One-armed hugs are like one-handed clapping. They may look like the real thing, but they don't mean much.

4. A hugger shall not combine a hug with a tickle.

5. Huggers shall refrain from hugging when it would hold up the line in front of the fried chicken at all-you-can-eat buffets.

Hugs lasting less than one second are "huggettes."

6. A hugger shall let go when asked to do so (unless he or she is attending a convention of Velcro salespeople and letting go is not an option).

7. While there is no set time limit on a hug, it is important to note that hugs lasting longer than two hours (other than as stated above) might be symptomatic of Lockarm Disease. Similar to Lockjaw, Lockarm prevents its victims from releasing hugs on their own. In more serious cases, a hugectomy may be required.

Lockarm Disease: In more serious cases,
a hugectomy may be required.

Hugs to Remember

My most meaningful hug: _____

My most anticipated hug: _____

My most awkward hug: _____

My most needed hug: _____

My happiest hug: _____

My most celebratory hug: _____

My silliest hug: _____

My tightest hug: _____

My slightest hug: _____

My longest hug: _____

My shortest hug: _____

My favorite hug: _____

A Picture Is Worth a Thousand Hugs

A few years ago I put together a "hug photo album." I came up with the idea one day while thumbing through albums of old photographs. I noticed that I would pause whenever I came upon a picture of someone hugging someone else. These snapshots evoked such a warm feeling that I thought it would be wonderful if they were all in one book.

I was right. It's by far my favorite album to look through because of all the loving memories it evokes.

Wondering what to do with all those special hug photos? Why not make a hug album of your own?

Bill of Rights for Huggers

Amendment 1

Congress shall make no law prohibiting the freedom of the people to embrace, hug, or peaceably assemble in a group hug.

Amendment 2

The people shall have the inalienable right to meet and wrap arms.

Amendment 3

No soldier shall, in time of peace, be hugless; nor in time of war, but in a manner to be prescribed by law, each member of our armed forces shall be hugged upon demand.

Amendment 4

The right of the people to hug shall be secure in their persons, houses, papers, and effects, against unreasonable handshakes and ever-so-slight head nods.

Amendment 5

A hugger shall not have to testify against him- or herself if charged with violation of Section 48 of the Huggers' Code of Conduct (hugging without a license).

Amendment 6

Should the hugger be charged with such a violation of the Code of Conduct, he or she has a right to a speedy trial by a jury of hugging peers.

Amendment 7

Solitary confinement for a hugger is considered cruel and unusual punishment.

The Last Word on Hugging

66 Looking back,

I have this to regret,

that too often when I loved,

I did not say so. **99**

David Grayson

Huggers' Hall of Fame

A certain woman who attended my church loved to hug. Really hug. Sophia King wasn't a large woman, but her hug could squeeze the breath right out of you. After one of her hugs, it always took a few minutes for your blood to return to its unhampered, steady flow, but no one minded. When she hugged you, you knew you were loved. And that's a nice feeling.

Sophia has long since relocated to a different state, but to this day I still miss her hugs. There was nothing like arriving at church and being greeted by her. No matter what had happened to you that week, no matter how many things had gone wrong or how down you felt, a hug from Sophia always lifted your spirits.

And she was an equal-opportunity hugger. It didn't matter if you were male or female, young or old. She didn't care about the color of your skin or whether you believed the same as she did. Her hugs crossed all barriers.

If there were a Huggers' Hall of Fame, Sophia King would be my nominee. Who will you nominate?

Share hugging fun with the coupons and certificates on the following pages. (You can make copies or tear or cut them out.)

♥ **Huggers' Hall of Fame Nomination** ♥

In recognition
of a remarkable talent for hugging
and outstanding achievements
as a career hugger and human tourniquet,

_____

is hereby inducted
into the Huggers' Hall of Fame.

Signed_____

♥♥♥♥♥♥♥♥♥♥♥♥♥♥♥♥

H♥U♥G♥S♥ ♥ H♥U♥G♥S♥

H♥U♥G♥S♥

H♥U♥G♥S♥ ♥ H♥U♥G♥S♥

H♥U♥G♥S♥

H♥U♥G♥S♥ ♥ H♥U♥G♥S♥

H♥U♥G♥S♥

H♥U♥G♥S♥ ♥ H♥U♥G♥S♥

H♥U♥G♥S♥

H♥U♥G♥S♥ ♥ H♥U♥G♥S♥

♥♥♥♥♥♥♥♥♥♥♥♥♥♥♥♥

♥ Hug Prescription ♥

Diagnosis: Acute Hug Deficiency, final stages
Treatment: One hug every hour, as needed

_____

Attending Ph.D. (Plentiful Hugs Doctor)

♥ Hug Prescription ♥

Diagnosis: Acute Hug Deficiency, final stages
Treatment: One hug every hour, as needed

_____

Attending Ph.D. (Plentiful Hugs Doctor)

♥♥♥♥♥♥♥♥♥♥♥♥♥♥♥

H•U•G•S• ♥ H•U•G•S•

H•U•G•S•

H•U•G•S• ♥ H•U•G•S•

H•U•G•S•

H•U•G•S• ♥ H•U•G•S•

H•U•G•S•

H•U•G•S• ♥ H•U•G•S•

H•U•G•S•

H•U•G•S• ♥ H•U•G•S•

♥♥♥♥♥♥♥♥♥♥♥♥♥♥♥

♥ **Hug Coupon** ♥

The bearer of this coupon is
entitled to one
Burned Dinner Hug.

♥ **Hug Coupon** ♥

The bearer of this coupon is
entitled to one
Unwanted Weight Gain Hug.

♥ **Hug Coupon** ♥

The bearer of this coupon is
entitled to one
Speeding Ticket Hug.

♥ **Hug Coupon** ♥

The bearer of this coupon is
entitled to one
Bad Hair Day Hug.

♥ **Hug Coupon** ♥

The bearer of this coupon is
entitled to one
Broken Shopping Cart Hug.

♥ **Hug Coupon** ♥

The bearer of this coupon is
entitled to one
Fender Bender Hug.

♥♥♥♥♥♥♥♥♥♥♥♥♥♥♥♥♥♥♥♥♥

H·U·G·S· ♥ H·U·G·S·

H·U·G·S·

H·U·G·S· ♥ H·U·G·S·

H·U·G·S·

H·U·G·S· ♥ H·U·G·S·

H·U·G·S·

H·U·G·S· ♥ H·U·G·S·

H·U·G·S·

H·U·G·S· ♥ H·U·G·S·

♥♥♥♥♥♥♥♥♥♥♥♥♥♥♥♥♥♥♥♥♥

♥ **Hug Coupon** ♥

The bearer of this coupon is
entitled to one
"The Kids' School
Principal Called" Hug.

♥ **Hug Coupon** ♥

The bearer of this coupon is
entitled to one
Load of White-Turned-Pink
Laundry Hug.

♥ **Hug Coupon** ♥

The bearer of this coupon is
entitled to one
Mother-in-Law Visiting
for the Weekend Hug.

♥ **Hug Coupon** ♥

The bearer of this coupon is
entitled to one
Stuck in Traffic and the Car Air
Conditioner Quit Hug.

♥ ♥ ♥ ♥ ♥ ♥ ♥ ♥ ♥ ♥ ♥ ♥ ♥ ♥ ♥ ♥

H♥U♥G♥S♥ ♥ H♥U♥G♥S♥

H♥U♥G♥S♥

H♥U♥G♥S♥ ♥ H♥U♥G♥S♥

H♥U♥G♥S♥

H♥U♥G♥S♥ ♥ H♥U♥G♥S♥

H♥U♥G♥S♥

H♥U♥G♥S♥ ♥ H♥U♥G♥S♥

H♥U♥G♥S♥

H♥U♥G♥S♥ ♥ H♥U♥G♥S♥

♥ ♥ ♥ ♥ ♥ ♥ ♥ ♥ ♥ ♥ ♥ ♥ ♥ ♥ ♥ ♥

♥ Hug Specialist Certification ♥

Howard University of Hugs
hereby awards the title of

Hug Specialist
to

_____

upon satisfactorily completing _____ hours of Hug Studies

and demonstrating responsible and enthusiastic

Hug Behavior above and beyond the call of duty.

This award is presented on the _____ day of _____, in

the year _____.

_____

President of Howard University of Hugs

♥♥♥♥♥♥♥♥♥♥♥♥♥♥♥♥♥

H•U•G•S• ♥ H•U•G•S•

H•U•G•S•

H•U•G•S• ♥ H•U•G•S•

H•U•G•S•

H•U•G•S• ♥ H•U•G•S•

H•U•G•S•

H•U•G•S• ♥ H•U•G•S•

H•U•G•S•

H•U•G•S• ♥ H•U•G•S•

♥♥♥♥♥♥♥♥♥♥♥♥♥♥♥♥♥

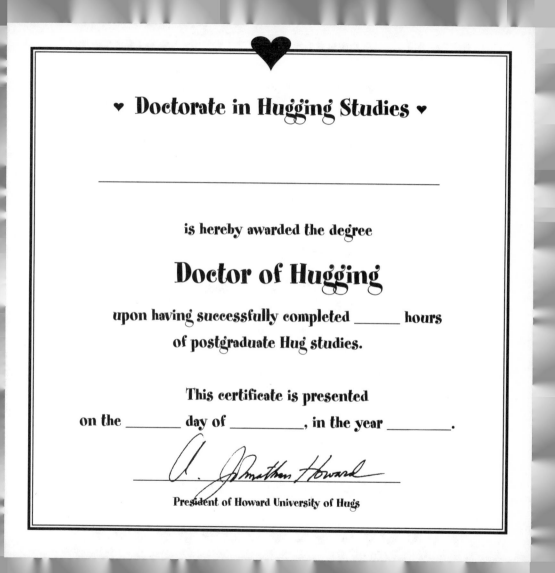

♥ **Doctorate in Hugging Studies** ♥

_____

is hereby awarded the degree

Doctor of Hugging

upon having successfully completed _____ hours
of postgraduate Hug studies.

This certificate is presented

on the _____ day of _____, in the year _____.

_____

President of Howard University of Hugs

♥♥♥♥♥♥♥♥♥♥♥♥♥♥♥♥♥♥

H♥U♥G♥S♥ ♥ H♥U♥G♥S♥

H♥U♥G♥S♥

H♥U♥G♥S♥ ♥ H♥U♥G♥S♥

H♥U♥G♥S♥

H♥U♥G♥S♥ ♥ H♥U♥G♥S♥

H♥U♥G♥S♥

H♥U♥G♥S♥ ♥ H♥U♥G♥S♥

H♥U♥G♥S♥

H♥U♥G♥S♥ ♥ H♥U♥G♥S♥

♥♥♥♥♥♥♥♥♥♥♥♥♥♥♥♥♥♥

66 We are each of us angels

with only one wing,

and we can only fly

embracing each other. **99**

Luciano de Crescenzo

Look for these other *Hugs* books:

Hugs for Women on the Go

Hugs for Heroes

Hugs for Women

Hugs for Sisters

Hugs for Grandma

Hugs for Friends

Hugs for Girlfriends

Hugs for New Moms

Hugs for Mom

Hugs for Daughters

Hugs for Grads

Hugs for Kids

Hugs for Teens

Hugs for Teachers

Hugs for Those in Love

Hugs for the Hurting

Hugs for Grandparents

Hugs for Dad

Hugs for the Holidays

Hugs to Encourage and Inspire